BUT SHE WAS BORN TO FLY

Poems for His Daughters

Shantrell Genese Williams

Shantrell Genese Williams is the author and copyright owner of all poems in this book. The following poems were previously published: Ode to Mothers, Aunts, Sisters, and Cousins © 2019, Chasing the Impossible © 2020, and Bird Songs © 2021.

Unless otherwise notated, scriptures are taken from the *King James Version* of the Bible. Direct quotations of scripture in poems are italicized.

Scriptures notated as (ASV) are taken from the *American Standard Version* of the Bible.

Scriptures notated as (WEB) are taken from the World English Bible®.

Scriptures notated as (NASB) are Scripture quotations taken from the (NASB®) New American Standard Bible®, Copyright © 1960, 1971, 1977, 1995, 2020 by The Lockman Foundation. Used by permission. All rights reserved. www.lockman.org

But She Was Born to Fly: Poems for His Daughters
Copyright © 2021 by Shantrell Genese Williams
All rights reserved. No part of this book may be reproduced, or stored in a retrieval system, or transmitted in any form or by any means, electronic, mechanical, photocopying, recording, or otherwise, without express written permission of the publisher.

ISBN: 978-1-7375720-0-8

Cover art by Katie Klopot of Katie's Canvas.

Published by Shantrell Genese Williams

*This book is dedicated to my sister Cynthia,
and to all my sisters in Christ who know there's more.*

Contents

Preface

How Can I? / 2
Fear / 3
Everything Is Fine / 4
Fallen Cares / 5
Waiting / 6
Stirring / 8
Where the Healing Starts / 9
Out on a Limb / 11
Spreading / 12
Twisted Roots / 13
Rahab: A Redemption Story / 14
Restored / 15
Stretch Marks / 17
But She Was Born to Fly / 18
All / 19
My Day / 20
Higher / 21
For His Glory / 22
Bird Songs / 23
A Love Like This… / 24
Ode to Mothers, Aunts, Sisters, and Cousins / 25
Chasing the Impossible / 26

Afterword / 27
Notes / 28
About the Author / 29

Preface

This book came out of a desire God placed in my heart to encourage His daughters. The verse that He gave me as I was seeking Him about whether to write this book is Luke 22:32, "But I have prayed for you, that your faith will not fail; and you, when you have turned back, strengthen your brothers" (NASB). Of course, I would replace "brothers" with sisters, but the principle is still the same. It can be summed up by what Jesus said in Matthew 10:8, "Freely you received, freely give" (NASB).

I did not have a particular theme in mind when I started writing and compiling the poems for this book, other than the aim to offer encouragement, but as I began to move forward, a theme of healing and restoration began to take shape. I believe this is God's heart for His daughters, and according to Scripture, it is certainly part of Jesus's ministry (See Luke 4:18), and Jesus always does what pleases the Father (See John 8:29). So, my prayer for you as you read this book is that you are encouraged and strengthened because you see our Father as the One who heals and restores.

One final note before you start: Although the poems in this book were written for God's daughters, it comes with an open invitation to all women. God invites all women to be His daughters through faith in His Son Jesus as Lord and Savior. So, if you aren't one of God's daughters, let's take care of that right now before we go any further! Just pray this simple prayer of faith from your heart:

God, I confess that you sent your Son, Jesus, to die for my sins and that You raised him from the dead so that I could have life in him. Your word says that everyone who calls on the Name of the Lord shall be saved (Acts

2:21). So Jesus, I call on you now. I repent of my sins and I ask you to come into my heart to be my Savior and Lord forever. Jesus, I now have new life in you and I belong to you. I am a child of God!

If you just prayed that prayer, welcome to the family! I gladly call you my sister in Christ! You have just been born again, so now it's time to fly!

'For I will restore you to health and I will heal you of your wounds,' declares the Lord, 'Because they have called you an outcast, saying: "It is Zion; no one cares for her."'

Jeremiah 30:17 (NASB)

How Can I?

Born to fly,
yet sit I
in the shallow end of life.
Wearied with frustrations.
Mired in situations.
Caught up in constant strife.
Want to break free;
I know there's more for me
than this barren place I find myself in.
How can I
spread wings and fly
when my heart is broken from within?

Fear

Fear,
you told me, "Don't even try;
girls like you weren't meant to fly."
Locked away in this opened cage,
the lies I believed setting the stage
for the woman I've become.
This woman I keep trying to outrun.
Running in circles, tripping over *weak and beggarly* things;
freedom just beyond the reach of these broken wings.[1]

Everything Is Fine

Everything is fine,
right?
Everyone just play your part,
while our lives are falling apart.
A thousand little pieces
lay fallen on the floor;
swept under the rug
because no one needs to know
that we are broken.
That we are hurting inside,
just on the other side
of the white picket fence.
Erected facades
to cover the shame and self-loathing;
like hiding in the garden
behind fig leaf clothing,
trying to keep the leaves from blowing away,
as they inevitably do.
How foolish we are to think
that our brokenness won't show through,
as long as we just keep saying,
"Everything is fine."

Fallen Cares

Invisible tethers
weighing down feathers,
taking on a world's fallen cares.
Building nests in thistles and thorns;
countenance fallen, looking forlorn.
Forgot that He's counted the very number of my hairs.

Waiting

There she sits,
perched on this broken limb;
bearing the weight
of so many yesterdays.
Wearied wings;
ruffled feathers.
A thousand reasons why
now is not the right time
to fly.
So, she sits.
Waiting…
Perched on this broken limb,
bearing the weight
of all those yesterdays,
swallowing up her tomorrows.
Because now is not the right time
to fly.

*As an eagle stirs up its nest,
and hovers over its young,
He spread His wings, He caught them,
He carried them on His pinions.*

Deuteronomy 32:11 (NASB)

Stirring

Seeds of promise
stirring in my dormant heart.
Unspoken dreams;
forgotten wishes upon distant stars.
Awakened by a Love
that never forgets;
beyond the limits of time,
eternity in our hearts He sets.[2]

Where the Healing Starts

He broke your heart;
his words cut deep into your soul.
Or the words he never spoke
created the hole
that left you feeling empty inside.
Broken men
leaving broken lives behind.
You reached up for love
but left with wounds
that have festered over time.
The child is now hidden
beneath a blanket of years;
covering up pain
and masking over fears
that threaten to expose.
But I see you there,
pretending to have it all together
and pretending not to care,
when you do.
I see the child,
who once reached up for love,
now reluctant to reach up for Me;
feeling unworthy of love
and distrusting Who I said I will always be.
Will you let Me in?
Into the hidden places of your heart?
Where the hurting never stops;
where the healing needs to start.
You say you belong to Me,
affirming that I sent My Son into the earth,
but you don't know Me as a Good, Loving Father,
distracted by the one who sowed into your birth.
Let Me be the Father
that he didn't know how to be.

Will you forgive his brokenness
so that you can be free?
Free to receive this love
that I so dearly long to give;
free to love yourself,
free to finally live.

Out on a Limb

Too far gone.
This broken record
replaying all my wrongs,
till Truth shined His light on all that was dim,
and mercy met me here
out on a limb.

Spreading

Spread your wings wide
in My Beloved,
and fly.
Plunge the depths;
soar the heights.
Open your heart
to truth that sets you free.[3]

Twisted Roots

Living in trees
I never meant to plant.
Twisted roots
buried deep
within the chambers of my heart,
feeding on lies
subtly disguised
as a better way to fly.
Casting down the lies I used to believe;
uprooting the hold of these broken trees,
so now I can truly fly.[4]

Rahab: A Redemption Story[5]

Did they see you?
Did they even care to
look into your eyes,
as they took pieces of your life
for a price
they could never fully pay?
Or did they just look away,
because they could never have seen you
even if they'd tried?
Your heart hidden, surrounded like walls
surrounding the heart of a city about to fall.
When you heard the knock at your door
did you think it was like all the other nights before?
Men looking for satisfaction
in the arms of the dissatisfied.
But this time it would be more than an empty exchange;
the entire narrative of your life was about to change,
and maybe you knew that.
Letting down your guard,
you opened your heart,
risking everything to save the ones you loved.
This would be your defining moment of redemption.
Choosing to trust in a God you didn't know,
that scarlet cord
tied discreetly from inside your window.
But that's not even the best part of your story.
Could you have even imagined
that God would use your life
as a backdrop to His greatest display of glory?
Through the redeemed life of a prostitute,
who chose to answer a call,
came the life of the Messiah,
Who came to save us all.

Restored

Broken pieces
gathered
in the One
broken for me.
His precious oil flowing down,
saturating these broken pieces
I let fall to the ground.
Coming together
at the voice of my cry
like dry bones in a valley.
I will breathe.
I will rise.
I will fly.

"Sing, barren, you who didn't give birth; break out into singing, and cry aloud, you who didn't travail with child: for more are the children of the desolate than the children of the married wife," says Yahweh. "Enlarge the place of your tent, and let them stretch out the curtains of your habitations; don't spare: lengthen your cords, and strengthen your stakes. For you will spread out on the right hand and on the left; and your offspring will possess the nations and settle in desolate cities. Don't be afraid, for you will not be ashamed. Don't be confounded, for you will not be disappointed. For you will forget the shame of your youth. You will remember the reproach of your widowhood no more."

Isaiah 54:1-4 (WEB)

Stretch Marks

Growing into this place,
as deep calls unto deep.[6]
Stretched beyond natural limits.
Birth pains of promise…the appointed time;
marks of greatness left behind.

But She Was Born to Fly

Don't get upset
when I refuse to see myself
as less than Whose I am,
or when I won't let you
systematically clip my wings
to keep me grounded
and focused on earthly things.
Should I apologize for wanting to fly
when that is what I was born to do,
or can I dim the brightness of my light
that will inevitably come shining through?
No, I will not and I shall not
ever be less than Whose I completely am.
Even if you never really see me
and my need to fly, you never truly understand.

All

I know who I am.
And I will be all of who I am.
I will fly.
Yes, even soar.
High above the tallest trees,
as they bend and sway
in awe of me.
This beautiful recreation
of God Most High;
the crowning glory of His creation,
who was born to fly.

My Day

Today is the day.
My day.
The sun is shining
and there's not a cloud in the sky.
The birds are singing,
and I know they're singing just for me.
The air is light and I breath in deeply,
filling my nostrils
with the sweet aroma of white gardenias
and the distinctive fragrance of fresh cut grass.
Gentle breezes wash over my sun-bathed skin,
telling the heat it can go no further.
Vivid colors of pinks, purples, and reds
adorn the tops of crepe myrtle trees,
surrounding me in a canvas of summer's finest hour.
I am entertained by a company of butterflies
dancing through the air
in rhythm to a symphony of cicadas.
Their crescendo drowning out the noise
of every worry and care.
I waited all winter for this moment.
I waited so long,
at times I thought this day would never come.
Times when my hopes seemed to be buried
under a blanket of fallen leaves,
and life felt like it was frozen in time
as days got shorter
and darkness celebrated the light it had conquered,
if only for a season.
But the season did change
and hopes were uncovered,
as life continued its onward march
and darkness gave way to the Risen Son.

Higher

The sensation
of this *rushing mighty Wind*,
washing over my Son-soaked skin.[7]
Lifting me higher,
and higher,
and higher.
Soaring carefree on eagle's wings;
a bird's eye view to see how He sees.
Carried by this *rushing mighty Wind*
to places eyes have yet to see.

For His Glory

How shall I boast
in what I was created to do?
I may spread my wings,
but it's not just to be seen by you.
These brightly colored feathers,
a brilliant reflection of the Light.
These wings molded into His image;
for His glory I take my flight.

Bird Songs

I woke up this morning
to pray;
as the birds sang praises to God,
I sang my own.

A Love Like This…

I want to curl up in You the way I curl up on the sofa on a chilly day, wrapped in my favorite throw.

I want to linger in Your embrace like I do when the one I love pulls me into his arms.

I want to listen to You sing over me the way the birds serenade the rising sun when I awake in the morning.

I want to drink You in the way I slowly sip on a hot cup of coffee with hazelnut creamer.

I want to savor Your presence the way I do a piece of my mother's world-famous (at least in my world) coconut pie.

I want to bask in Your love the way I bask in the sun on the first warm day of spring.

I want to shout for joy at the awesomeness of Your glory the way I scream at the top of my lungs when my favorite team hits a buzzer-beating shot!

Or when my heart is heavy, I want to let my tears fall into Your cupped hands, like drops of rain cascading down a window pane.

I want to laugh with You at the impossible the way I laugh so hard that my side hurts when my sister and I share an inside joke.

And I want to gaze at Your untold beauty the way I gaze in awe at the painted canvas of leaves draped over the North Carolina mountains in the fall.

Ode to Mothers, Aunts, Sisters, and Cousins

To the women of my family -
the Soft-Spoken, the Sassy, the Strong, and the Sure -
I wear you like *a coat of many colors*
draped over a life that came out of you.[8]

Your eyes have seen years slip away
into the good ole days,
days when simple pleasures eased burdens
that were not uniquely your own.
Your heart has felt the indescribable joy
of new and hopeful beginnings,
and has been weighed down by the sorrow
of untimely and tragic endings.
Your hands have reached out to give,
and give,
and give,
and give.
Your best meal prepared.
Your wisdom shared.
Your life poured out.
You wouldn't have had it any other way.
For your feet have walked down roads
you would have rather not traveled,
but when you reached the end
you looked back and showed others the way.

So, to the women of my family -
the Soft-Spoken, the Sassy, the Strong, and the Sure -
I proudly wear you like *a coat of many colors*
draped over a life that came out of you.

Chasing the Impossible

The girl
who once caught lightening bugs
to hide away in jars
is chasing the impossible
and catching distant stars.

Afterword

Every good thing God has for His children is in Jesus. Ephesians 1:3 says, "Blessed be the God and Father of our Lord Jesus Christ, who has blessed us with every spiritual blessing in the heavenly places in Christ" (NASB). This is the place of healing and restoration, and it comes through an understanding of who we are in Christ. My book Beholding Jesus is a devotional that invites you to look into the "mirror" of the face of Christ, through His word, with the aim of helping you receive a fresh revelation of who Jesus is and who you are in Him. If this book spoke to you, I recommend that you continue this journey of healing and restoration by reading Beholding Jesus.

Thank you for allowing me to encourage you with the truths that have encouraged me in my own journey of healing and restoration. Sister, never forget that we were born to fly!

Notes

[1] Galatians 4:9
[2] Ecclesiastes 3:11 (ASV)
[3] See John 8:31-32
[4] See 2 Corinthians 10:4-5
[5] See Joshua Chapter 2 and Matthew 1:1-17
[6] Psalm 42:7
[7] Acts 2:2
[8] Genesis 37:3

About the Author

I want to live a life
that makes people talk,
maybe even gawk.
Average is so over-rated;
I'd rather be the definition
of unanticipated
when I walk into a room.
Nope, you didn't see this coming.
Didn't realize what I was becoming,
or rather, what I've always been.
You thought you'd already heard this story
from beginning to end.
But this is the beginning of greater works
that some ears haven't yet heard;
this is the culmination of a dream
birthed in the heart of a girl
told to, "Speak a word..."

Other Books by the Author

Beholding Jesus: A Poetry Devotional
Let the Church Be His Church
Poems for Night Seasons
What Manner of Love

Contact the Author:

shantrellgenese@gmail.com

Made in the USA
Monee, IL
30 September 2023